I love reading

Amazing Motorbikes

by Frances Ridley

Contents

Words in **bold** are explained in the glossary.

Copyright © ticktock Entertainment Ltd 2008
First published in Great Britain in 2008 by ticktock Media Ltd.,
Unit 2, Orchard Business Centre, North Farm Road,
Tunbridge Wells, Kent, TN2 3XF

We would like to thank: Penny Worms, Alix Wood and the National Literacy Trust.

ISBN 978 1 84696 776 4

Printed in China

A CIP catalogue record for this book is available from the British Library.

Picture credits: b=bottom; c=centre; t=top; r=right; l=left
All images Car Photo Library - www.carphoto.co.uk, except: Action Plus: 15tr, 21tr;
Alvey and Towers: 20-21c, b/c cl

Every effort has been made to trace the copyright holders, and we apologise in advance for any
unintentional omissions. We would be pleased to insert the appropriate acknowledgements
in any subsequent edition of this publication.

Aprilia RSV Mille R

The RSV Mille R was launched in 2002. The R stands for 'Racing'.

The Mille R is big, fast and comfortable. It has a top speed of 270 km/h.

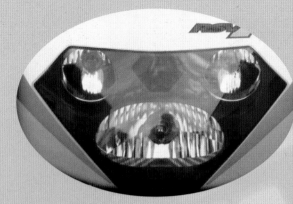

The Mille R
has a triple
headlight.

It also has special brakes
at the front. You can
stop very quickly
if you need to.

Buell XB9R Firebolt

The Firebolt is very light for a
motorbike – it only weighs 175 kg.

Its powerful engine makes it very fast.
It has a top speed of 209 km/h.

The Firebolt is an unusual bike. It has a hollow frame to store fuel.

Its **exhaust** is underneath the bike, not on the side.

Honda CBR1100XX Blackbird

The Blackbird has a huge engine. It also has a **streamlined** shape.

It can **accelerate** from 0 to 209 km/h in just 11 seconds.

In 2001, a **turbo-charged** Blackbird did a wheelie at 321 km/h!

It has special brakes. They slow down the front and back tyres at the same time.

Kawasaki Ninja ZX-12R

The Ninja ZX-12R has a top speed of 305 km/h. Its streamlined shape helps the bike go fast.

The Ninja has a scoop
under the headlight.
The scoop forces air
into the engine.
This drags
in extra
fuel and
gives the
Ninja more power.

The big fuel tank
lets you travel
a long way
before you need
more fuel.

Harley-Davidson V-Rod

Harley-Davidson launched the V-Rod in 2002. It's much lighter and faster than other Harley-Davidson bikes.

The V-Rod's fuel tank is under the seat. This leaves room for air intakes, giving the V-Rod more power.

This badge shows that
Harley-Davidson has made
bikes since 1903.

Ducati 999S

There are three kinds of Ducati 999. The 999S has a top speed of over 274 km/h and can accelerate from 0 to 100 km/h in less than 3 seconds.

It has won three world championships in superbike racing.

The seat, fuel tank and footrests all move so the rider can make it more comfortable.

MV Agusta F4 SPR Senna

Ayrton Senna was a famous Formula One racing driver. He died in a race. The Senna motorcycle is named after him.

The twin
headlights
are stacked
on top of
each other.

The Senna is a
beautiful bike.
MV Agusta only made
300 of them.

Suzuki GSX1300R Hayabusa

Suzuki launched the Hayabusa in 1998. It was the fastest road bike of its time. A hayabusa is a Japanese bird of prey.

The GSXR100 is the Hayabusa's little brother. It has better acceleration than the Hayabusa because it is lighter.

Suzuki GSXR1000

The Suzuki GSXR1000 is a very powerful racing bike. It is used in many superbike world championship races.

Its top speed is 306 km/h!

20

Part of the Suzuki GSXR1000 is made of **titanium.** This makes it so light it can accelerate from 0 to 97 km/h in just under 2.5 seconds.

Yamaha YZF-R1

Yamaha is famous for making motorcycles. The R1 can do 120 km/h in first **gear** and over 160 km/h in second gear!

The YZF-R6 is one of Yamaha's most popular bikes. It is small and light but not as fast as an R1.

This is the YZF-R1 2007. It can accelerate from 0 to 97 km/h in under 3 seconds. Its top speed is over 304 km/h.

Glossary

accelerate   To make the bike go faster.

exhaust   A pipe that takes engine gases away from the rider.

gears   Toothed wheels used to change the speed of a bike.

streamlined   A smooth shape that cuts through wind and helps a bike go faster.

titanium   A very hard, but very light metal.

turbo-charged   When air is forced into the engine, dragging in fuel for more power.

Index